This Python Isn't a Snake

What Are Coding Languages and Syntax?

by Brian P. Cleary

illustrations by Martin Goneau

Millbrook Press • Minneapolis

Computers are devices
that can process information—

called data—such as
numbers, words, and facts.

They're found in watches, smartphones, cars, and microwaves as well;

in ATMs and tablets filled with apps.

Coding is the process of developing instructions

so computers can perform a given task,

like telling us the weather forecast,

letting us play games,

or a thousand other things
that we might ask.

But where does all that code come from?
Who writes it all—and how?

People write the code,
and you can too!

A code helps make new software or build an app or site,

so you can tell computers what to do.

Just as we speak **languages** like
Arabic or Spanish,
a coder, too, needs **languages** to tell
computers what to do by using
**Java, Alice, Python,
Ruby, Scratch,** and **C++** as well.

These and other **languages** we've listed in the back are chosen based on what the coder's making:

an app that teaches you to dance or helps you write a song

or a website built for perfect pizza baking.

Lua is a **language** used in many classic games like Star Wars: Battlefront or Angry Birds.

And **Python**, **Java**, and **C++**
are often used for apps

by the brightest and the
nerdiest of nerds.

Syntax is a fancy word referring to arranging our words and phrases in a certain way.

It helps us so our meaning
will be clearly understood

in sentences we either
write or say.

"Josh ate almost all the candy"
doesn't mean the same
as "Josh almost ate all the candy."

See?

The order of these same six words—the way that they're arranged—
can change the meaning quite remarkably.

Using proper **syntax**
also counts when writing code.
The order of the words and punctuation

will help you to deliver the results
you're looking for

with no mix-up or discombobulation.

Depending on the **language**, there
are different ways to help
our cat here to express this
simple thought.

Maybe with a little help, you'll try it on your own

and have some fun with all that you've been taught!

So what are languages and syntax?

Do you know?

Coding is fun! And best of all, anyone can do it! All you need is a computer or tablet, an internet connection, and a willingness to try.

As you read in this book, computer code can be written in a variety of languages. It's helpful to pick one language to begin with, and after you start feeling comfortable with that language, you may become interested in checking out some other languages. Different languages are good for different purposes.

Here are some common languages that you may want to check out:

- Scratch
- Hopscotch
- Alice
- Python
- Ruby
- Java
- Lua

Each language has its own syntax, which is the order of the instructions. Languages that use block coding, such as Scratch and Alice, help make syntax easy, because you can drag and drop "blocks" of code to write your program. Start with something small and short, and as you become more comfortable, you can write longer, more complex programs. Don't worry if you don't get everything right on your first try. The more you practice, the easier it will be!

Want to learn more?

Check out these great resources!

Books

Funk, Josh. *How to Code a Sandcastle*. New York: Viking Books for Young Readers, 2018. Follow along as Pearl and her robot friend Pascal figure out how to build a sandcastle by using code. They break down the problem into small steps and use concepts including loops and sequences to achieve their goal.

Loya, Allyssa. *Disney Coding Adventures: First Steps for Kid Coders*. Minneapolis: Lerner Publications, 2019.
Computational thinking is the first step to coding. In this book, kid coders can start on the basics in a fun and easy way by learning about algorithms, bugs and errors, loops, and conditionals alongside Disney characters.

Robinson, Fiona. *Ada's Ideas: The Story of Ada Lovelace, the World's First Computer Programmer*. New York: Abrams Books for Young Readers, 2016.
This picture book biography introduces trailblazer Ada Byron Lovelace. She loved math and science, and she created the first computer program—even before electronic computers existed.

Websites and Apps

Code.org
https://code.org
This site has lots of resources for anyone who wants to start coding—including students and their teachers. Check out the "Projects" tab to see what other kids have done and take a look at the code for these projects.

Scratch Jr.
https://www.scratchjr.org
This simple, block-based programming language was created especially for early elementary students who don't have any previous coding experience. It runs on both iPads and Android tablets.

Find activities, games, and more at www.brianpcleary.com

ABOUT THE AUTHOR & THE ILLUSTRATOR

BRIAN P. CLEARY is the author of the best-selling Words Are CATegorical® series, as well as the Sounds Like Reading® series, the Poetry Adventures series, and several others. He is also the author of *Crunch and Crack, Oink and Whack! An Onomatopoeia Story* and *The Sun Played Hide-and-Seek: A Personification Story*. He lives in Cleveland, Ohio.

MARTIN GONEAU is the illustrator of many books, including quite a number in the Words Are CATegorical™ series. When he is not drawing, he enjoys playing video games and learning how to code. He lives in Trois-Rivières, Québec, with his lovely wife and his two sons.

Thank you to technical expert Michael Miller for reviewing the text and illustrations.

Millbrook Press
A division of Lerner Publishing Group, Inc.
241 First Avenue North
Minneapolis, MN 55401 USA

For reading levels and more information, look up this title at www.lernerbooks.com.

Main body text set in Chauncy Decaf Medium 27/36. Typeface provided by the Chank Company.
The illustrations in this book were created in Adobe Photoshop using a Wacom Cintiq Pro 16.

Library of Congress Cataloging-in-Publication Data

Names: Cleary, Brian P., 1959– author. | Goneau, Martin, author.
Title: This python isn't a snake : what are coding languages and syntax? / Brian P. Cleary, Martin Goneau.
Description: Minneapolis, MN : Millbrook Press, a division of Lerner Publishing Group, Inc., [2019] | Series: Coding is CATegorical | Includes bibliographical references and index. | Audience: Ages 5–9. | Audience: Grades K to 3.
Identifiers: LCCN 2018022635 (print) | LCCN 2018026401 (ebook) | ISBN 9781541543850 (eb pdf) |
    ISBN 9781541533066 (lb : alk. paper) | ISBN 9781541545571 (pb : alk. paper)
Subjects: LCSH: Programming languages (Electronic computers)—Juvenile literature.
Classification: LCC QA76.7 (ebook) | LCC QA76.7 .C56 2019 (print) | DDC 005.2—dc23

LC record available at https://lccn.loc.gov/2018022635

Manufactured in the United States of America
1-44875-35725-8/15/2018